First published in 2024 by OH
An Imprint of HEADLINE PUBLISHING GROUP

2 4 6 8 10 9 7 5 3 1

Disclaimer:

Cataloguing in Publication Data is available from the British Library

ISBN 978-1-03542-093-3

Compiled and written by: Malcolm Croft
Editorial: Saneaah Muhammad
Designed by: Andy Jones
Project manager: Russell Porter
Illustration by: Ryan Adley
Production: Arlene Lestrade
Printed and bound in China

MIX
Paper | Supporting
responsible forestry
FSC® C104740

HEADLINE PUBLISHING GROUP
An Hachette UK Company
Carmelite House, 50 Victoria Embankment, London EC4Y 0DZ

www.headline.co.uk   www.hachette.co.uk

POP
CHAMELEO

FS
www.fs

THE LITTLE GUIDE TO
MILEY CYRUS

POP CHAMELEON

UNOFFICIAL AND UNAUTHORIZED

CONTENTS

INTRODUCTION

In February 2024, America's favourite teenage girl-next-door turned wild child, Miley Cyrus, received recognition from her peers – finally! – after 15 years. Miley won two Grammy Awards – golden trophies that cemented her status as a true global icon. After creating eight studio albums, selling over 55 million singles and 20 million albums worldwide and enough tongue-poking to last two lifetimes, Miley is now on equal terms with her idols Madonna, Dolly Parton and Debbie Harry and has become an inspiring LGBTQ+ role model to her global fanbase of supporters, young and old.

As the daughter of country music superstar Billy Ray Cyrus – and born in 1992 with the name Destiny Hope – Miley was always destined to do great things. When, at the age of 13, Miley hit the big time as Disney's pre-teen princess on *Hannah Montana*, her future fate as a run-of-the-mill pop star seemed all but sealed.

However, when it comes to Miley Cyrus, nothing is that predictable. For the next decade, Miley pulled off a mixture of mischief, mirages and magic to constantly confound and challenge popular culture, shapeshifting her styles and sounds to suit her ever-evolving moods and becoming its most innovative, inventive and unescapable asset in the process. As unpredictable as she is in your face, Miley Cyrus is, without a doubt, the voice of her generation, and she's got the bangerz to prove it.

This little guide to Miley is serious about Cyrus. It's packed with all the wonderful wit, wisdom and wisecracks her worldwide fans have come to love over the years. Taken from interviews throughout her near-20-year career, *Pop Chameleon* reveals the real Miley Cyrus, one candid, controversial and classic quote at a time.

Let's party…

CHAPTER
ONE

BREAKOUT

Growing up the daughter of US country superstar and future television co-star Billy Ray Cyrus, the fledgling actor and musical artist born Destiny Hope was profoundly inspired by her father and was managed by her mother, Tish.

When she took her first steps into the spotlight as her alter-ego – the bewigged teenage pop superstar Hannah Montana – Miley's career was a dream about to come true. Perhaps…

I was born right when 'Achy Breaky' came out. I remember Dad always being on tour, he was gone a lot. But that was cool for me, it allowed me to be independent and work my way to acting and singing by myself, and not just by following my dad's lead. 🙷

Miley, on her father's fame and her independence, interview with Ian Youngs, *BBC Newsbeat*, October 14, 2008.

It does get frustrating having the cameras on me all the time, because if I make mistakes, the whole world knows about it.

Miley, on being in the spotlight 24/7, interview with Audrey Fine, *Seventeen*, January 3, 2008.

Sometimes I'll watch myself
on TV and ask myself
'What am I doing? I am
the biggest geek.'

Miley, on watching *Hannah Montana*, interview with
Audrey Fine, *Seventeen*, January 3, 2008.

That's what a star is: they're different. A celebrity is different. There can't be a thousand Miley Cyrus'es – that doesn't make me special.

Miley, on being different, interview with Bruce Handy, *Vanity Fair*, April 28, 2008.

"

I felt it was her destiny to bring hope to the world.

"

Billy Ray Cyrus, on Miley's birth name,
Ellen DeGeneres Show, 2007.

Miley's given name was Destiny Hope. However, she legally changed her name to Miley Ray Cyrus in 2008.

She chose Miley due to her childhood nickname – Smiley.

No matter how long what I'm doing here lasts, I want to be a songwriter for the rest of my life. I love it and it's my escape. I just hope Breakout showcases that – more than anything – I'm a writer.

Miley, on her debut album *Breakout* and song writing, interview with Cortney Harding, *Billboard*, June 27, 2008.

Sometimes I just want to go to the mall and be able to shop around. Then, when I go out, I realize I don't have a normal life. My world is not normal.

Miley, on being normal, interview with Robin Roberts, *Good Morning America*, July 20, 2008.

I was too small and too young to fit in with the group they had already casted. But after a year had gone by, they called me back and said they wanted to give me another chance now that I had grown up. And the rest is herstory.

Miley, on her *Hannah Montana* audition journey, originally auditioning for the role of Lily, interview with Kara Nesvig, *Teen Vogue*, November 1, 2023.

I liked being in the Disney universe because I didn't know anything else. I knew I was getting to live what I wanted to do. I think now that I'm older now, I realize that's a lot to put on a kid.

Miley, on the struggles behind starring in the Disney Channel's *Hannah Montana*, interview with Kara Nesvig, *Teen Vogue*, November 1, 2023.

There's so much I don't remember about being a child entertainer because it was so much to keep in my brain. I didn't realize how much pressure I was under and how that shaped me until much later.

Miley, on the pressure of playing Hannah Montana, interview with Jessica Pressler, *Harper's Bazaar*, July 13, 2017.

Hannah Montana was not a character. That wasn't what the show is about. It was about a normal girl with a fucking wig on. Everything was always in me. The concept of the show, it's me. I've had to really come to terms with that and not be third person about it.

Miley, on the reality of being Hannah Montana, interview with Brittany Spanos, *Rolling Stone*, December 4, 2020.

> **"**
> I'm a crazy chiquita.
> I'm nuts.
> **"**

Miley, on her wild side, interview with Marshall Heyman, *Teen Vogue*, April 5, 2009.

A mistake is only really a mistake if you don't learn from it. When I'm 30, am I going to be thinking about things that seem massive right now? Probably not.

Miley, on making mistakes, interview with Marshall Heyman, *Teen Vogue*, April 5, 2009.

I was attracted to girls way before I ever was attracted to guys. When I was 11 years old, I used to think that Minnie Mouse was super fucking hot, which is so good I ended up on Disney, so my chances with Minnie went up by like 100.

Miley, on her gender fluidity, interview with Alexandra Cooper, Barstool Sports' *Call Her Daddy* podcast, August 13, 2020.

I was told for so long what a girl is supposed to be from being on *Hannah Montana*. I was made to look like someone that I wasn't, which probably caused some body dysmorphia because I had been made pretty every day for so long. And then when I wasn't on that show, it was like, 'Who the fuck am I?'

Miley, on *Hannah Montana* defining her femininity, interview with Kara Nesvig, *Teen Vogue*, November 1, 2023.

I think why people loved the show was because Hannah Montana felt real. And that's because I was under there.

Miley, on her authenticity when playing the role of Hannah Montana, interview with Anthony Mason, *CBS Sunday Morning*, October 29, 2017.

From the time I was 11, I was told, 'You're a pop star! That means you have to be blonde, and you have to have long hair, and you have to put on some glittery tight thing.' Meanwhile, I'm this fragile little girl playing a 16-year-old in a wig and a ton of makeup. It was like *Toddlers & Tiaras*. I had fucking flippers.

Miley, on being molded into a child star, interview with Allison Glock, *Marie Claire*, August 12, 2015.

People are like, 'You're sixteen, why would you write your life story?' But in the business, I'm in, I have lived a life that some people who are in their sixties haven't lived. I've gone through a lot and seen a lot. But I still have a lot to learn.

Miley, on writing her 2009 autobiography *Miles To Go*, interview with Marshall Heyman, *Teen Vogue*, April 5, 2009.

I just wanted to be on TV. They'll probably kill me for saying it, but I was probably the least paid person on the *Hannah Montana* cast because I didn't know any better. I was just like, 'I can be on Disney!'

Miley, on fame over fortune, interview with Manda Fitzsimons, *Elle*, September 27, 2016.

I probably started writing songs when I was 10 years old. I started a band called Blue Roses, and our first song was 'Pink Isn't a Color'. That was my first band. It was a girl rock band.

Miley, on her earliest song writing, interview with Brittany Spanos, *Rolling Stone*, December 4, 2020.

"

When I was 11 or 12, my friends were starting to kind of like tell me what they were doing with guys and I didn't really understand it, so I got most of my girlfriends to hook up with me. The first time I ever hooked up with anyone was with a girl. Two of them.

"

Miley, on her first hook up, interview with Alexandra Cooper, Barstool Sports' *Call Her Daddy* podcast, August 13, 2020.

When my peers are having these experiences and accepting themselves because of something that I demonstrated while they were a kid, that's when I go, 'Shit, I fucking am Hannah Montana.'

Miley, on the enduring influence and inspiration of Hannah Montana, interview with Brittany Spanos, *Rolling Stone*, December 4, 2020.

I have 200 or 300 friends, but I probably trust four. I've learned who I can really trust. When I read something in the tabloids and it's from an 'insider', I want to know who thinks they're on the 'inside'. Because I can count on one hand the people who really know me.

Miley, on trust and friendships, interview with Laurie Sandell, *Glamour*, March 29, 2009.

You don't show your personality by what you wear – it's about how you present yourself, by always having a smile.

Miley, on expressing personality through a smile, interview with Marshall Heyman, *Teen Vogue*, April 5, 2009.

"

My job is to be a role model, and that's what I want to do, but my job isn't to be a parent. My job isn't to tell your kids how to act or how not to act, because I'm still figuring that out for myself. Your kids are going to make mistakes whether I do or not. That's just life.

"

Miley, on being a role model, interview with Amy Larocca, *Harper's Bazaar*, January 6, 2010.

I think at some point during everyone's life, you finally figure yourself out. I haven't even done that yet.

Miley, on understanding herself, interview with Laurie Sandell, *Glamour*, March 29, 2009.

Every career thing I do can't be perfect and sometimes my decisions are wrong. The minute I stop making mistakes is the minute I stop learning... and I've definitely learned a lot.

Miley, on learning from her mistakes, interview with John Hiscock, *The Telegraph*, March 25, 2010.

We're halfway into the last season and it's kind of bittersweet for me. It's like my security blanket, my comfort zone: I know that's where I'm going to be from 8.30am to 6pm. I've always had the show to lean on, and to not have it to lean on in the future will be different for me, so who knows?

Miley, on the ending of *Hannah Montana* in 2011 and her plans for the future, interview with John Hiscock, *The Telegraph*, March 25, 2010.

66

I would not change the
way I grew up for anything.
But I am really overwhelmed.
My career is a huge
responsibility. I went to the
Oscars for the first time
when I was 13.

99

Miley, on life as a child star, interview with Laurie Sandell,
Glamour, March 29, 2009.

It was so embarrassing, but I couldn't leave. And I was crying, begging my mom, 'You're going to have to put the tampon in. I have to be on set.'

Miley, on having her first period while on the *Hannah Montana* set, interview with Allison Glock, *Marie Claire*, September 2015.

CHAPTER
TWO

THE CLIMB

From 2006–2011, Miley became America's new favourite pop star in disguise – Hannah Montana, a pre-teen dream for the Disney Channel.

A ratings hit, the show introduced Miley to a global audience and greeted her with high acclaim and praise for her singing and acting. But it also caused an identity crisis for its burgeoning star, causing Hannah and Miley to go their own ways – for now…

The minute I had sex for the first time, I was like, 'I can't put the fucking wig on again!' It got weird. It felt ridiculous. I was grown up.

Miley, on growing up beyond *Hannah Montana*, interview with Kara Nesvig, *Teen Vogue*, November 1, 2023.

I was embarrassed. I think that just makes me even more relatable. I don't think people will look at me any differently because they're like, 'You know what, I'm going to do stupid stuff too, and I'm going to make mistakes, and that's fine.' It still hurts when I think about it, but you know what? It doesn't mean that you can't move on.

Miley, on the infamous and controversial 2008 *Vanity Fair* "nude" cover, interview with Cortney Harding, *Billboard*, June 27, 2008.

"

The smartest thing I ever did was to put my debut album on a double disc. I wasn't valued at the time like Hannah was. But the voice behind Hannah was always me.

"

Miley, on releasing *Meet Miley Cyrus* as a double-CD, one side of Miley as Hannah Montana and the other side as herself, interview with Kara Nesvig, *Teen Vogue*, November 1, 2023.

Miley hit the big time in March 2006 after she was cast as the lead character in Disney Channel's *Hannah Montana*, playing none other than Hannah Montana herself.

The show soon became Disney's highest-rated series of all time. It ran for four seasons until 2011. Miley was just 13 when she was cast as Hannah.

The type of tachycardia
I have isn't dangerous.
It won't hurt me, but it does
bother me. There is never
a time onstage when
I'm not thinking about
my heart.

Miley, on her tachycardia, a condition that causes
a faster heart rate, from her autobiography
Miles to Go, 2010.

I started touring as both Hannah Montana and as myself. I think that's probably what's a little bit wrong with me now! I mark that up to doing some extreme damage in my psyche as an adult person.

Miley, on her debut double tour as herself and Hannah Montana, interview with Anthony Mason, *CBS Sunday Morning*, October 29, 2017.

I'm not ashamed of Hannah
Montana anymore. It's pretty
cool when you hear Cardi B was
listening to Hannah Montana
when she was in high school.
That shit makes me happy.

Miley, on Hannah Montana's enduring legacy, interview
with Molly Lambert, *Elle*, July 11, 2019.

If you think dancing on top of
an ice-cream cart with a pole
is bad, then go check what
90 per cent of the high schoolers
are really up to.

Miley, on her notorious and now-famous "Party in the
USA" performance at the Teen Choice Awards 2009,
interview with Kevin Sessums, *Parade*, March 21, 2010.

The concept of the show is that when you're this character, when you have this alter ego, you're valuable. You've got millions of fans, you're the biggest star in the world. And then when I looked like myself, when I didn't have the wig on anymore, no one cared about me, I wasn't a star anymore. So, that was drilled into my head. Like, without being Hannah Montana, no one cares about you. And that was the concept. Talk about an identity crisis.

Miley, on playing Hannah Montana and having an identity crisis, interview with Allison Hagendorf, *Rock This* podcast, March 2021.

America feels like my aunt telling me, 'You've grown up so much, and we don't want to see you grow up!'

Miley, on America's attitude towards Miley's rebellious phase after leaving *Hannah Montana*, interview with Anthony Mason, *CBS Sunday Morning*, October 29, 2017.

People have known me since I was so young, they think they know me. I heard so many comments like, 'We just want Miley back.' But you can't tell me who that is. I'm *right* here.

Miley, on fans believing they know Miley, interview with Jessica Pressler, *Harper's Bazaar*, July 13, 2017.

If I wear something revealing, people go, 'Well, that's not Christian.' And I'm like, 'Yeah, I'm going to go to hell because I'm wearing a pair of really short, white shorts.' Suddenly, I'm a slut. That's so old school.

Miley, on her faith and her fashion, interview with Kevin Sessums, *Parade*, March 21, 2010.

At some point, I'm definitely, I'm getting the wig out of storage.

Miley, on the potential future return of Hannah Montana, interview with Nashville's *107.5 The River* radio station, October 2020.

I am literally open to every single thing that is consenting and doesn't involve an animal, and everyone is of age. Everything that's legal, I'm down with. I'm down with any adult – anyone over the age of 18 who is down to love me. I don't relate to being boy or girl, and I don't have to have my partner relate to boy or girl.

Miley, on her fluid sexuality and being open to anything, interview with *PAPER Magazine*, June 2015.

I had to evolve because Hannah was larger than life, larger than me. I felt like I was never going to amount to the success of Hannah Montana. That's how Lil Nas X actually knew of my dad. He grew up watching *Hannah Montana* and said, 'I want to do a song with Robby Ray [Billy Ray Cyrus].' That's literally what happened.

Miley, on the viral hit "Old Town Road" featuring Lil Nas X and Billy Ray Cyrus, interview with Brittany Spanos, *Rolling Stone*, December 4, 2020.

It's so much easier to know who you are when there aren't a thousand people telling you who they think you are. I felt like I was really figuring myself out. Usually, I have someone whispering in my ear, but I was on my own.

Miley, on leaving *Hannah Montana*, interview with Amy Larocca, *Harper's Bazaar*, January 6, 2010.

When you're a pop star you always have 'people'. You always hear, 'My people will call your people,' but you can't let your people talk for you all the time because you're the only person who knows yourself and what you truly want.

Miley, on speaking for herself, interview with John Hiscock, *The Telegraph*, March 25, 2010.

My job first is to entertain and do what I love, and if you don't like it, then change the channel. I'm not forcing you to watch me. I'm not forcing you to talk about me.

Miley, on being an entertainer, interview with Kevin Sessums, *Parade*, March 21, 2010.

Miley has a tattoo of Johnny Cash's autograph that Cash – a friend of her father – gave to Miley when she was a little girl.

The tattoo reads "I'm in your corner".

I remember telling my mom I admire women in a different way. And she asked me what that meant. And I said, I love them like I love boys. It was so hard for her to understand. She didn't want me to be judged and she didn't want me to go to hell. But she believes in me more than she believes in any God. I just asked for her to accept me. And she has.

Miley, on coming out to her mom during her teen years, interview with *PAPER Magazine*, June 2015.

I want to be the cool chick that everyone wants to be friends with. I want the people who watch my shows or watch my videos to be like, 'She looks like the most fun person to hang out with ever. I want to be that girl's best friend. I want to party with her.'

Miley, on being fun, interview with Josh Eells, *Rolling Stone*, September 27, 2013.

The adrenaline that you have after a show – it's not really the singing that affects your voice as much. It's afterwards, you're totally on and it's really hard to get that sleep. You stay up, talking all night. Later, the talking all night turned into smoking all night.

Miley, on the changing sound of her voice over the years, interview with Joe Rogan, *The Joe Rogan Experience* podcast, September 2, 2020.

I was so influential in kids' lives that I was like America's nanny. Like, 'Just sit your kids in front of me and I'll teach them how to be a good person.' Which maybe backfired on the American godparent.

Miley, on her influence over American teens, interview with Zach Baron, *Vanity Fair*, February 21, 2019.

To stay updated, to keep educating myself, to never stop learning, to continue evolving and be conscious of the evolution happening around me, too. Keeping up with the next generation, looking at what they're doing and what they're interested in. What happens if you don't do that? You turn into Billy Ray Cyrus, who doesn't have Wi-Fi.

Miley, when asked "What advice would you give yourself 10 years from now?", interview with Hattie Collins, *Vogue*, June 4, 2021.

People get told that it's a bad thing to change. People will tell me, 'You've changed.' And that's supposed to be derogatory. But you are supposed to change all the time.

Miley, on her forever changing and evolving mindset, interview with Jessica Pressler, *Harper's Bazaar*, July 13, 2017.

The first record that I ever made as myself – not as Hannah Montana, the first record I ever made as Miley Cyrus – I did most of that record in that house.

Miley, on the importance of the house* that burned down in the Woolsey wildfires, interview with Zach Baron, *Vanity Fair*, February 21, 2019.

* It was, as a bizarre coincidence, the same house that Liam Hemsworth bought years later, and where the married couple lived.

Both of my parents are big stoners.
I remember one time the producers
on *Hannah Montana* started screaming
at me because they thought that
I was smoking pot in the dressing
room. And I was like, 'I'm not
fucking smoking pot in the dressing
room. Go knock on my fucking
dad's door.' It was my dad.

Miley, on her dad smoking pot, interview with
Zach Baron, *Vanity Fair*, February 21, 2019.

I grew up on a tour bus.
I went with my dad everywhere.
He turned it into a playhouse
for us. They had some stairs
you could go down to get under
the bus where the luggage
would be, and he created
a place for me and my brother
to go and play and imagine
and dream.

Miley, on touring with her dad as a child, interview
with Rick Owens, *Interview Magazine*, June 4, 2021.

I carried some guilt and shame around myself for years because of how much controversy and upset I really caused. Now that I'm an adult, I realize how harshly I was judged.

Miley, on her wild and rebellious phase after her Disney years, interview with Tomás Mier, *Rolling Stone*, May 18, 2023.

Right now, when people go to iTunes and listen to my old music, it's so irritating to me because I can't just erase that stuff and start over. My last record I feel so disconnected from – I was 16 when I made it. When you're in your 20s, you just don't really know that person anymore.

Miley, on the artistic transition she experienced during the production of *Bangerz*, interview with Jason Chester, *Billboard*, June 14, 2013.

Joan Jett told me about the first time she played 'I Love Rock 'n' Roll' and Clive Davis said, 'No one wants to see a girl with short hair and a guitar.' Now any time anyone tells me no, I'm like, 'Well, you know what? People told fucking Joan Jett that they didn't want "I Love Rock 'n' Roll."' That's my clapback for everything.

Miley, on responding to short-sighted opinions, interview with Molly Lambert, *Elle*, July 11, 2019.

No wonder I went crazy for a couple of years.

Miley, on being managed by her mother, Tish, and working daily on set with her father, Billy Ray, during the *Hannah Montana* years, interview with Zach Baron, *Vanity Fair*, February 21, 2019.

CHAPTER
THREE

TWERK IT

Welcome to the Miley-high club!

Global stardom arrived with Miley's first true musical masterpiece *Bangerz* (2013) and its global hit songs "Wrecking Ball" and "We Can't Stop".

It was to be the artist's finest hour (so far) but also the beginning of her wild child era, a period that dominated headlines worldwide with many famous, controversial and media-baiting cultural milestones – while also expressing Miley's desire to be completely different.

Will the real Miley Cyrus please stand up?

America is just so weird in what they think is right and wrong.

Miley, on American values, interview with Josh Eells, *Rolling Stone*, September 27, 2013.

I hear what you say but I'm gonna do the opposite of it. Because you're old and you're a man, and I'm young and I'm a girl and I know that's right. I've got to make sure that I'm the voice of my generation. I think that I'm allowing girls to be really free with their sexuality.

Miley, on ignoring the advice from her managers about her look and behavior, interview with *Marie Claire*, December 3, 2015.

I want *Bangerz* to be the biggest record in the world. I've given everything to get here, even friends and family and relationships. I've just put this music first.

Miley, on the making of *Bangerz*, interview with Jason Chester, *Billboard*, June 14, 2013.

No one is talking about the man behind the ass. It was a lot of 'Miley twerks on Robin Thicke,' but never, 'Robin Thicke grinds up on Miley.' They're only talking about the one that bent over. So obviously there's a double standard.

Miley, on twerking on Robin Thicke at the 2013 VMAs, interview with Josh Eells, *Rolling Stone*, September 24, 2013.

I'm 20 years old and I want to
talk to the people that are up
all night with their friends.
'We Can't Stop' is based on a
true story of a crazy night
I had. When I heard the song
for the first time, it captured
exactly what I was living.

Miley, on "We Can't Stop", interview with
Jason Chester, *Billboard*, June 14, 2013.

I was creating attention for myself because I was dividing myself from a character I had played.

Miley, on separating herself from Hannah Montana during her wild period following the success of *Bangerz* and "Wrecking Ball", interview with Giles Hattersley, *Vogue*, May 18, 2023.

A lot of people wanted to try to make me the white Nicki Minaj. That's not what I'm trying to do.

Miley, on being the next Nicki Minaj, interview with Jason Chester, *Billboard*, June 14, 2013.

I'm listening to it 20,000 times to make sure it's perfect. I have to make sure every detail is perfect. There are albums that people still are listening to, like Michael Jackson's *Bad*, because it's so fucking dope. I want people to listen to *Bangerz* like that. I want to make sure my record is the best it can be. I'm trying to set a new standard for pop music.

Miley, on perfecting *Bangerz*, interview with Josh Eells, *Rolling Stone*, September 27, 2013.

When I did 'Wrecking Ball' nobody saw my pain, of me looking directly into the camera, breaking the wall, crying, reaching out. Everyone just remembers me getting naked.

Miley, on the raw emotion behind the song "Wrecking Ball", interview with Brittany Spanos, *Rolling Stone*, December 4, 2020.

Miley has sold more than 20 million albums worldwide and more than 55 million singles.

Her most successful album is *Bangerz* (2013), which has sold more than seven million copies worldwide.

"

I'm not the same person I was six months ago. I'm not even the same person I was two weeks ago.

"

Miley, on her constant evolution, interview with Jason Chester, *Billboard*, June 14, 2013.

I want to start as a new artist. I consider *Bangerz* my first, really.

Miley, on recreating her career with *Bangerz*,
interview with Jason Chester, *Billboard*, June 14, 2013.

Everyone, you're welcome.
I took all the slaps for you!
Everything that anyone could
have been mad at, I've done it
all, so nothing seems that bad
compared to all the things
I've done.

Miley, on being a scapegoat for all of society's problems,
interview with Anthony Mason, *CBS Sunday Morning*,
October 29, 2017.

You're so fearless when you get yourself dressed when you're a kid. You don't think about what someone will think of you or what they'll judge. It's just about expression and how you feel that day. There's a fearlessness. And so, when I get dressed, I try to kind of think like my inner child, and be genuine and authentic in whatever I'm wearing.

Miley, on her fearless fashion choices, interview with Hattie Collins, *Vogue*, June 4, 2021.

The media likes to have my hair or what I look like be the point of reference for my sanity. 'Hair's long and blond, she's sane right now. She cannot be fucked up on drugs. It's when her hair is painted or she's growing out her armpit hair that she's on drugs.'

Miley, on the media defining her mental state based on her hair, interview with Brittany Spanos, *Rolling Stone*, December 4, 2020.

"

I gotta keep doing stuff that's really crazy. I need my own *Rolling Stone* column where every issue it's just something crazy I do.

"

Miley, on her crazy behavior during her wild era, interview with Josh Eells, *Rolling Stone*, September 24, 2013.

To me, fun is any time I feel
I really reach my full potential.
When the glass ceiling breaks.
That's fucking fun for me.

Miley, on how she likes to have fun, interview with
Brittany Spanos, *Rolling Stone*, December 4, 2020.

One time I went backstage at Disneyland, and Peter Pan was smoking a cigarette. And I was like, 'That's me. That's the kind of dreams I'm crushing.' That's how everyone felt with the bong video, but I'm not a Disney mascot. I'm a person.

Miley, on the leaked footage of her smoking a salvia bong in 2010 and being a role model, interview with Molly Lambert, *Elle*, July 11, 2019.

The 'We Can't Stop' video made my mom really angry. She knew the voice and talents that I could showcase. She was like, 'What the fuck? You have the biggest song. Can you just make it about the song? Why do you have to make it about being a stripper?'

Miley, on the "We Can't Stop" music video, interview with Brittany Spanos, *Rolling Stone*, December 4, 2020.

I didn't realize that it was going to shift me into truly being my own person. It changed my life. I felt like that divide, that boundary was very clear.

Miley, on *Bangerz* taking a wrecking ball to her old image, interview with Anthony Mason, *CBS Sunday Morning*, October 29, 2017.

A couple of years ago, it looked like I was living some fairy tale. It really wasn't. At that time, my experimentation with drugs and booze and the circle of people around me was not fulfilling or sustainable or ever going to get me to my fullest potential and purpose.

Miley, on her experimental phase in the mid 2010s, interview with Brittany Spanos, *Rolling Stone*, December 4, 2020.

At the 2013 VMAs when everyone in the entire world knew that I had dressed up as a teddy bear and danced with Robin Thicke and everyone talked about it for a really long time. I woke up and, you know, it was on every news channel. And everyone had their opinion about it. At that time, it was like, 'Oh my God, she's dressed as a bear with no pants on.' Bears don't wear pants!

Miley, on her now-famous 2013 VMA performance, interview with Anthony Mason, *CBS Sunday Morning*, October 29, 2017.

The song 'Fly on the Wall' was about the media [I received] at that time. They were already starting to label me as 'America's Sweetheart Gone Wrong.' I was thinking, 'If you could only be a fly on the wall. It's worse than you can imagine.' Or better, I guess.

Miley, on the extensive media attention she received, interview with Brittany Spanos, *Rolling Stone*, December 4, 2020.

2013 was the year of Miley Cyrus. She was Google's most searched person, according to their annual Zeitgeist report.

Miley came first, followed by Drake, Kim Kardashian, Justin Bieber and Beyoncé!

People were so shocked by some of the things that I did at the VMAs. It should be more shocking that when I was 11 or 12, I was put in full hair and makeup, a wig and told what to wear by a group of mostly older men.

Miley, on her "outrageous" 2013 VMA performance and *Hannah Montana*, interview with Jessica Pressler, *Harper's Bazaar*, July 13, 2017.

There's a release of dopamine that gets dumped into your skull when people are raving about you or when you walk by a magazine stand and you're on every cover. However, you do get to a point where sales numbers and headlines don't do the same chemical reaction to your brain as they do in the beginning.

Miley, on the addictive qualities of fame, interview with Brittany Spanos, *Rolling Stone*, December 4, 2020.

I think everyone would have given anything to be me at that moment, because I was being one hundred percent true to myself and not many people can say that.

Miley, on the famous 2013 MTV Video Music Awards, interview with Kyle Buchanan, *Cosmopolitan*, October 26, 2013.

When I was on my *Bangerz* tour, it was hard for my soul to walk out and see people with their arms crossed. I walked out so many nights feeling judged. You're at my show, why are you here to judge me?

Miley, on her crossover period and her 2013–2014 *Bangerz* tour, interview with Manda Fitzsimons, *Elle*, September 27, 2016.

With *Bangerz*, the pop culture moments almost eclipsed the music itself.

Miley, on the iconic cultural moments that accompanied the release, promotion and tour of *Bangerz*, interview with Brittany Spanos, *Rolling Stone*, December 4, 2020.

Everything that I'm doing is supposed to be life and art imitating each other, and so everything has always been honest at that time. When I did 'Party in the USA', that was how I felt. When 'We Can't Stop' came out, I was living that life. It's not like every day I went to the set to act. When it comes to music, I've always been honest.

Miley, on practicing what she preaches, interview with Kyle Buchanan, *Cosmopolitan*, October 26, 2013.

Singing 'Wrecking Ball', about feeling completely broken and shattered. Everyone's suffering is different, even everyone's threshold of pain. I wear a lot of glitter and I wear a lot of armor, and I also wear my heart on my sleeve and it gets broken a lot.

Miley, on the meaning behind "Wrecking Ball", interview with Allison Hagendorf, *Rock This* podcast, March 2021.

I'm not saying you need to take a break *because* you're crazy. I'm saying you need to take a break so you can *be* crazy.

Miley, on taking a break from life to truly live, interview with Derek Blasberg, *Harper's Bazaar*, September 16, 2013.

I feel like an underdog in a cool way. Society wants to shut me down.

Miley, on the headlines, scrutiny and criticism she received for her behavior during the *Bangerz* era, interview with Kyle Buchanan, *Cosmopolitan*, October 26, 2013.

Not only was culture changed, but my life and career were changed forever.

Miley, on the famous 2013 MTV Video Music Awards and twerking on Robin Thicke for "Blurred Lines", interview with Lauren Rearick, *Teen Vogue*, March 1, 2018.

My parents are proud of my work. My dad doesn't care what I do on stage – he gets my being controversial. In his day, he would be wearing tank tops and Reeboks to the Grammys when all the other country singers wore cowboy boots.

Miley, on her relationship with her parents, interview with Lena de Casparis, *Elle*, September 21, 2015.

Everything is so chaotic and crazy right now and it's so much all at once, but I'm living for it. I'm just having the best time ever, and everything's falling into place like it's supposed to. Even people who want to hate on me, they can't even shut down the fact that I'm literally what everyone is talking about. I'm on top right now.

Miley, on the global and phenomenal success of the *Bangerz* album and tour, interview with Lauren Rearick, *Teen Vogue*, March 1, 2018.

When people started complaining about the 2013 MTV awards show, I was like, 'Have you never seen the "Blurred Lines" video?' And what if I hadn't done that performance? The VMAs would have been bad. They would have been missing something. The show was kind of making fun of how serious the pop industry is.

Miley, on the backlash she received for the 2013 MTV Video Music Awards, interview with Kyle Buchanan, *Cosmopolitan*, October 26, 2013.

I know what I'm doing. When I'm dressed in that teddy bear suit, I think that's funny.
When I'm in that teddy bear suit, I'm like a creepy, sexy baby.
I know I'm shocking you.

Miley, on being deliberately controversial, interview with Josh Eells, *Rolling Stone*, September 27, 2013.

I worked more when I was a kid than I'd ever allow myself to do now. I'm living out my rebellious teenage whatever now because I couldn't when I was younger.

Miley, on the reasons behind her rebellious phase following the success of *Bangerz*, interview with Tavi Gevinson, *Elle*, May 1, 2014.

I don't actually walk around all day twerking with my tongue out dressed as a teddy bear.

Miley, on her reputation following the aftermath of the notorious 2013 VMA performance, interview with Chi Chi Izundu, *BBC Newsbeat*, November 12, 2013.

There were so many things
I have had to say sorry for that
I wasn't sorry about.

Miley, on the constant pressure to apologize for her behavior, interview with Tavi Gevinson, *Elle*, May 1, 2014.

I feel like the luckiest woman doing what I do. But being a pop star is kind of the dumbest shit of all time. I'm kind of embarrassed that I got paid to shake my ass in a teddy bear costume.

Miley, on her ambivalent feelings about her career, interview with Lena de Casparis, *Elle*, September 21, 2015.

Your mind can be your army or your enemy – and you have to learn how to control that.

Miley, on her life philosophy, interview with Kyle Buchanan, *Cosmopolitan*, October 26, 2013.

I think weed is the best drug on earth. One time I smoked a joint with peyote in it, and I saw a wolf howling at the moon.

Miley, on her love of smoking weed, interview with Josh Eells, *Rolling Stone*, September 27, 2013.

I have guys and girls that come to me and say, 'The only reason I'm able to admit that I'm gay is because you've made me feel like that's okay.' That gives me a big purpose – a reason to wake up in the morning that's bigger than putting on my fucking feathers and my little outfits.

Miley, on meaning more to her fans than just music and fashion, interview with Tavi Gevinson, *Elle*, May 1, 2014.

I had something called Reinke's Oedema, which, when my doctor told me about it, he said, 'No one shy has this. This is for abuse of the voice. This is for people that talk way too fucking much and usually, this happens when you're like in your 60s or 70s.'

Miley, on the changing sound of her voice over the years, interview with Joe Rogan, *The Joe Rogan Experience* podcast, September 2, 2020.

CHAPTER
FOUR

THE FULL MILEY

The singer-songwriter's desire to experiment with her sound, vision, sexuality and lifestyle dominated her post-*Bangerz* period, transforming the musician into something more than just an artist: she blossomed into her generation's greatest pop-culture chameleon.

To celebrate, she offered up several versions of herself, all of whom were devoured by her insatiable legion of loyal fans. This is the full Miley… in all her glory.

"

When I walk into a room, people may think, 'Okay, she gets her tits out.' But they also think, 'But she's got a fucking sick voice,' and that's all I care about.

"

Miley, on her wild style and iconic vocals, interview with Molly Lambert, *Elle*, July 11, 2019.

66

People ask me how I stay happy and sane. I never Google myself.

99

Miley, on staying sane by distancing herself from the internet, interview with Tavi Gevinson, *Elle*, May 1, 2014.

I have that tendency to just let my wild fucking thoughts drive me.

Miley, on her impulsiveness, interview with Zach Baron, *Vanity Fair*, February 21, 2019.

I'm more extreme and badass than most guys, but that doesn't make me a boy. And the other night I wore a pink dress because I felt cute. I can bake a cupcake and then go play hockey.

Miley, on being the best of both worlds, interview with Lena de Casparis, *Elle*, September 21, 2015.

66

I try really hard to impress my band and crew. I don't want them to think I'm some dumb pop bitch.

99

Miley, on making a good impression with her peers, interview with Tavi Gevinson, *Elle*, May 1, 2014.

I think people, if they actually knew me, would be surprised at how normal I am. I'm definitely crazy but I'm normal. I am socially probably more acceptable than a lot of people in this industry because I've just always grown up around this and so I never have any kind of attitude.

Miley, on her reputation in the music industry and her normality, interview with Chi Chi Izundu, *BBC Newsbeat*, November 12, 2013.

I like the way being sexual makes me feel, but I'm never performing for men. They shouldn't compliment themselves to think that the decisions I'm making in my career would have anything to do with them getting pleasure. I don't think that because some guy thinks I'm hot he's going to buy my record.

Miley, on her power and sexuality, interview with Molly Lambert, *Elle*, July 11, 2019.

I was so embarrassed to be on the red carpet and so many of those fucking disgusting photographers would tell me to blow a kiss, and that's not me! I don't want to blow you a kiss. I didn't know what to do with my face, so I stuck my tongue out, and it became a rebellious, punk-rock thing.

Miley, on her signature facial expressions, interview with John Norris, *Billboard*, March 5, 2017.

A big part of my pride and my identity is being a queer person. In the same way I like to be genderless, I like feeling genre-less.

Miley, on her sexual and gender identity, interview with Zach Baron, *Vanity Fair*, February 21, 2019.

Mileyography:
Studio Albums

1. *Meet Miley Cyrus* (2007)
2. *Breakout* (2008)
3. *Can't Be Tamed* (2010)
4. *Bangerz* (2013)
5. *Miley Cyrus & Her Dead Petz* (2015)
6. *Younger Now* (2017)
7. *Plastic Hearts* (2020)
8. *Endless Summer Vacation* (2023)

Do people really think that I'm at home in a fucking apron cooking dinner?

Miley, on refusing stereotypical gender roles, interview with Molly Lambert, *Elle*, July 11, 2019.

> People stare at me anyway,
> but people stare at me
> a lot when I'm dressed as
> a fucking cat.

Miley, on her wacky fashion sense, interview with
John Norris, *Billboard*, March 5, 2017.

If you're hanging out with
Beyoncé, you're hanging
out with a goddess. She's
like a real queen. It's a
different realm. My thing
is kind of the opposite. My
shtick is I'm the homey.

Miley, on being down to earth, interview with Josh Eells,
Rolling Stone, September 27, 2013.

Miley High Club:
Top Ten Most Streamed Songs

1. "Flowers" (2023)
2. "Party in the USA" (2009)
3. "We Can't Stop" (2013)
4. "Nothing Breaks Like a Heart" (2019)
5. "Wrecking Ball" (2013)
6. "Angels Like You" (2020)
7. "Malibu" (2017)
8. "Prisoner" (featuring Dua Lipa) (2020)
9. "Midnight Sky" (2020)
10. "The Climb" (2009)

I have to ask myself,
'How am I going to create
real change?' and not just
fucking preach to the
choir anymore.

Miley, on making a difference through actions not words,
interview with John Norris, *Billboard*, March 5, 2017.

I've definitely felt like Ashley O…
I read it and was like, 'It's not
even if I'm interested or not. It's
just that no one can play this
because this is my life. Like, you
just took my life.'

Miley, on relating to and playing the character
Ashley O in the *Black Mirror* episode "Rachel, Jack and
Ashley Too", interview with Molly Lambert, *Elle*,
July 11, 2019.

I'm in a hetero relationship, but I still am very sexually attracted to women. People become vegetarian for health reasons, but bacon is still fucking good, and I know that.

Miley, on her fluid sexuality, interview with Molly Lambert, *Elle*, July 11, 2019.

Younger Now is a reflection of the fact that, yes, I don't give a fuck, but right now is not a time to not give a fuck about people. I'm giving the world a hug and saying, 'Hey, look. We're good – I love you.' And I hope you can say you love me back.

Miley, on *Younger Now* (2017) and trying to unite a divided America, interview with John Norris, *Billboard*, March 5, 2017.

"

Don't let this blonde hair fool you. I'm the one signing my checks.

"

Miley, on being the boss of her own life, interview with Molly Lambert, *Elle*, July 11, 2019.

Times are changing. I think there's a generation or two left, and then it's gonna be a whole new world.

Miley, on the future of popular culture, interview with Josh Eells, *Rolling Stone*, September 24, 2013.

"

At the end of the day, I'm a nice person. I take pride in the fact that I treat everyone well. There's no reason for anyone to ever come at me because I only want the best for everybody else. I don't ever throw shade at anyone.

"

Miley, on being undeserving of the online criticism she receives, interview with Kyle Buchanan, *Cosmopolitan*, October 26, 2013.

I hate the paparazzi – but when they're not sitting there waiting for you, you're like, 'Who's bigger news? Who are you trying to get a picture of?'

Miley, on her paradoxical relationship with paparazzi, interview with Josh Eells, *Rolling Stone*, September 27, 2013.

I hung out with way too many adults when I was a kid. So now I don't want to hang out with any adults. I've already done all the hard work. Now I can kind of fuck off.

Miley, on spending time with adults as a teenager, interview with Josh Eells, *Rolling Stone*, September 24, 2013.

I feel very gender-fluid. For a long time, I didn't understand my own sexuality. I would get really frustrated and think I'd never understand what I am, because I can't even figure out if I'm feeling more like a girl or boy. It took me talking to enough trans people to realize that I didn't ever have to decide on one.

Miley, on her gender fluidity, interview with *PAPER Magazine*, June 2015.

Ayahuasca was definitely one of my favourite drugs I've ever done. When I did it, I asked everyone else in the room, 'Did your entire life just change? Are you a new person?' They all looked at me and said, 'No.' And they're like, 'You're so extreme. Of course, you have to have the most extreme trip of all.'

Miley, on taking Ayahuasca, interview with Brittany Spanos, *Rolling Stone*, December 4, 2020.

When I look at retouched, perfect photos, I feel like shit. They lighten black girls' skin. They smooth out wrinkles. Even I get stuck on Instagram wondering, 'Why don't I look like that?' It's a total bummer. It's crazy what people have decided we're all supposed to be.

Miley, on the false reality of social media, interview with Allison Glock, *Marie Claire*, August 12, 2015.

I'm probably never going to be the face of a traditional beauty company unless they want a weed-smoking, liberal-ass freak. But my dream was never to sell lip gloss. My dream is to save the world.

Miley, on promoting cosmetic products, interview with Allison Glock, *Marie Claire*, August 12, 2015.

Miley's "fairy" godmother,
and career inspiration,
is Dolly Parton.

66

I watch people like Dolly.
Dolly knows what she is. She's
smart. She's not just a blonde
with big titties – she is a genius
under there.

99

Miley talking to *Rolling Stone* in 2013.

I didn't go all the way with a dude until I was 16. I ended up marrying the guy, so that's pretty crazy. He was the first guy I hooked up with, which I lied and said that he wasn't the first, so I didn't seem like a loser.

Miley, on her relationship with Liam Hemsworth, interview with Alexandra Cooper, Barstool Sports' *Call Her Daddy* podcast, August 13, 2020.

"

One of the reasons I got sober was I had just turned 26. I said, 'I got to pull my shit together before I'm 27, because 27 is the time you cross over that threshold into living or dying a legend.' I didn't want to join that club.

"

Miley, on the "27 Club", interview with Brittany Spanos, *Rolling Stone*, December 4, 2020.

When I introduced Joan Jett into the Rock and Roll Hall of Fame, I said, 'The reason I'm here tonight is because I want to fuck Joan.' Everyone laughed because they thought it was a joke. It wasn't.

Miley, on her idol, Joan Jett, interview with Allison Glock, *Marie Claire*, August 12, 2015.

I made Paul McCartney feel uncomfortable one time. I was inducting Joan Jett into the Rock and Roll Hall of Fame, and I went and introduced myself with nipple pasties on. He turned bright red, and that I really liked! I was so freaked out to meet Paul McCartney, that then he was freaked out to meet me! So, the roles just reversed.

Miley, on meeting Paul McCartney, interview with Anthony Mason, *CBS Sunday Morning*, October 29, 2017.

CHAPTER
FIVE

FLOWER POWER

In the 2020s, Miley emerged happy and healthy from heartbreak, home-burning and a hell-raising past.

Newly and creatively inspired, she won two Grammy Awards in February 2024 and recognition from her peers that she was more than just her headlines. This chapter focuses on Miley's happiness, philanthropy and present state of mind.

With her global icon status assured, where Miley goes next is anybody's guess. Only one thing is certain: this happy hippie has still got many miles to go…

This award is amazing, but I really hope it doesn't change anything because my life was beautiful yesterday. Not everyone in the world will get a Grammy but everyone in this world is spectacular so please don't think that this is important.

Miley, accepting her first Grammy "Record of the Year" award for "Flowers", *Grammy Awards*, 2024.

When we lost our house in Malibu, I lost everything. That trauma really affected my voice.

Miley, on the changing sound of her voice over the years, interview with Howard Stern, *Howard Stern Show*, December 4, 2020.

I'm introducing my audience, my generation, to everything that inspired me and created this cocktail of chaos that I am.

Miley, on the influences heard on *Plastic Hearts*, interview with Brittany Spanos, *Rolling Stone*, December 4, 2020.

Women are expected to keep the planet populated. And when that isn't a part of our plan or our purpose, there is so much judgment and anger that they try to make and change laws to force it upon you – even if you become pregnant in a violent situation. If you don't want children, people feel sorry for you, like you're a cold, heartless bitch who's not capable of love.

Miley, on stereotypical gender roles and choosing whether or not to have children, interview with Molly Lambert, *Elle*, July 11, 2019.

I grew up working on Sunset Boulevard where so many homeless people are. When I go back to my old stomping ground and see kids wearing Happy Hippie T-shirts, that makes me feel so much more proud than if I had seven Grammys sitting on the wall.

Miley, on the the positive impact of her youth homelessness foundation Happy Hippie, interview with Molly Lambert, *Elle*, July 11, 2019

"Getting married, for me, was one last attempt to save myself.

Miley, on getting married to Liam Hemsworth, interview with Brittany Spanos, *Rolling Stone*, December 4, 2020.

In the past two years, we've made some big progress, especially toward women and bodies. I don't even know if you really can slut-shame now. Is that even a thing? The media hasn't really slut-shamed me in a long time.

Miley, on being a former victim of slut-shaming, interview with Brittany Spanos, *Rolling Stone*, December 4, 2020.

The more that you love your own decisions, the less you need other people to love them.

Miley, on her philosophy for life and loving herself, interview with Anthony Mason, *CBS Sunday Morning*, October 29, 2017.

Even though it's not who
I am, I'm not afraid of who
I used to be.

Miley, on proudly claiming her past behaviors,
interview with Anthony Mason, *CBS Sunday Morning*,
October 29, 2017.

66

We've been doing the same thing to the Earth that we do to women. We just take and take and expect it to keep producing. And it's exhausted. It can't produce. We're getting handed a piece-of-shit planet, and I refuse to hand that down to my child. Until I feel like my kid would live on an Earth with fish in the water, I'm not bringing in another person to deal with that.

99

Miley, on having children during a climate crisis, interview with Molly Lambert, *Elle*, July 11, 2019

I just don't believe that everyone gets what they deserve. I know a lot of amazing people through Happy Hippie who are homeless – artists who are super talented who've never gotten a break. I fucking know that karma isn't real.

Miley, on her youth homelessness foundation Happy Hippie and karma, interview with Molly Lambert, *Elle*, July 11, 2019.

I tried to go to therapy a few times. And they treated me like I was everyone else who sits on the couch. They'd be like, 'Well, you probably feel paranoid because you're smoking weed.' And I reply, 'No, I feel paranoid because people are putting little drones in my backyard.'

Miley, on intrusive paparazzi drones*, interview with Molly Lambert, *Elle*, July 11, 2019.

* "One time I was naked on top of a fake horse when a drone showed up. And I'm like, 'Honestly, I couldn't have asked for a better time.' At least I wasn't sitting there drinking coffee, being boring."

I think I'm just figuring out who I am at such a rapid pace that it's hard for me to keep up with myself.

Miley, on her constantly shifting attitudes, styles and personalities, interview with Jessica Pressler, *Harper's Bazaar*, July 13, 2017.

Just because I got my tits out before doesn't make me less of a role model.

Miley, on being a role model, interview with
Jessica Pressler, *Harper's Bazaar*, July 13, 2017.

I don't give a fuck about being cool. I just want to be myself. And I think I show people that they can be themselves.

Miley, on being true to herself, interview with Jessica Pressler, *Harper's Bazaar*, July 13, 2017.

I would say it would have to be a cold day in hell for me to relapse on drugs. I would possibly take mushrooms.

Miley, on drug and drink sobriety and relapse, interview with Brittany Spanos, *Rolling Stone*, December 4, 2020.

66

I'm not sexually confused in any way. I'm very much pansexual. That just means everyone. It doesn't stop at girl, boy, or if someone's in a transition. I don't see people ever for who they were before who they are right now.

99

Miley, on her sexuality, interview with Manda Fitzsimons, *Elle*, September 27, 2016.

"

Just because you're an artist it doesn't give you an excuse to be an asshole.

"

Miley, on being an artist, interview with
Manda Fitzsimons, *Elle*, September 27, 2016.

In November 2018, Miley's home in Malibu, the one she shared with her then-husband Liam Hemsworth, burned to the ground during the Woolsey wildfire.

The fire destroyed 1,643 structures, killed three people and prompted the evacuation of more than 295,000 people.

Along with the house and all her possessions, Miley also lost two pet pigs, two horses, four cats and seven dogs.

The wildfires forced me out of my comfort zone, to find a new place to call home. All this shit I collected for all these years doesn't make me who I am. That doesn't amount to *me*.

Miley, on losing all her material possessions in the 2018 Woolsey wildfires, interview with Molly Lambert, *Elle*, July 11, 2019.

I want to get fucked up and live life to the fullest. But is it really living life to the fullest if you can't remember anything? 'Live fast, die young,' isn't really the goal.

Miley, on sobriety, interview with Brittany Spanos, *Rolling Stone*, December 4, 2020.

"

I don't have Instagram on my phone anymore. This chick at the office, I gave her my password. I'll send her a picture of me feeding the pig in a bikini: 'Can you post, like, "Fuck yeah, pigs!" or "High in a bikini!"' I don't want to scroll. I don't want to know what people are doing. I don't need to know who's got a new music video and who's got a new lipstick. It felt so commercial like I was always getting sold.

"

Miley, on distancing herself from social media, interview with Manda Fitzsimons, *Elle*, September 27, 2016.

I want to lay down a new stone for a path for the next generation of artists and philanthropists, the way that Debbie Harry has done for me. I'd like to be known as someone that created something that didn't quite exist, or that I delivered something that no one knew that they needed, but when they had it felt that they couldn't live without it. That's what I want as an artist.

Miley, on how she would like to be remembered, interview with Brittany Spanos, *Rolling Stone*, December 4, 2020.

I'm like the face of going out, and I never go out. All I want to do is yoga and hike and smoke weed.

Miley, on her party reputation, interview with Manda Fitzsimons, *Elle*, September 27, 2016.

"

I wear my empowerment at all times. I don't need to profess it.

"

Miley, on empowerment, interview with Giles Hattersley, *Vogue*, May 18, 2023.

If one of my friends doesn't see me for two or three weeks, they have to re-get to know me in a way. My soul will still be the same, but everything around me can be different and I won't dress the same and maybe different kinds of people will be around.

Miley, on her shape-shifting styles and passions, interview with *PAPER Magazine*, June 2015.

I've have been very experimental. I've been with a lot of different kinds of like dudes and chicks. I've been with like super femme girls and girls that make me feel more femme. The main thing for me is that someone has to bring something that is elevating my life. That's in all my relationships, not just my sexual relationships.

Miley, on her experimentation with sex and relationships, interview with Alexandra Cooper, Barstool Sports' *Call Her Daddy* podcast, August 13, 2020.

I never need to be a master at the craft of tricking an audience. It will set itself on fire all by itself.

Miley, staying true to herself and her fans, interview with Giles Hattersley, *Vogue*, May 18, 2023.

I have such male energy. I associate with male energy more because I feel their sense of power.

Miley, on male energy, interview with Zach Baron,
Vanity Fair, February 21, 2019.

I wrote 'Flowers' in a really different way. The chorus was originally: 'I can buy myself flowers, write my name in the sand, but I can't love me better than you can.' It used to be more, like, 1950s. The song is a little fake it till you make it… which I'm a big fan of.

Miley, on her Grammy-award winning feminist anthem "Flowers", interview with Giles Hattersley, *Vogue*, May 18, 2023.

Miley's "Flowers", released in January 2023, has become her biggest hit and her first No.1 smash since "Wrecking Ball" in 2013.

"Flowers" became the most streamed song in a single day on Spotify with more than 10 million steams!

I might be No. 1 now, but No. 2 is on its way. Everything is seasonal. A lot of headlines recently have said, 'This is Miley's moment.' And I'm like, 'That's exactly what it is. It's a moment. And it will be over.'

Miley, on her return to global success in 2023 with "Flowers" and *Endless Summer Vacation*, interview with Giles Hattersley, *Vogue*, May 18, 2023.

I should not be worth the amount I am while people live on the street. Nothing I do will justify that. But I have so much influence as a pop star, it's important I use it.

Miley, on her Happy Hippie homeless foundation, interview with Lena de Casparis, *Elle*, September 21, 2015.

I have such a healthy and sexy relationship with recklessness right now. I can say yes to anything. It would take something really fucking crazy for me to say no.

Miley, on her recklessness, interview with Rick Owens, *Interview Magazine*, June 4, 2021.

A trying time is no time to quit trying.

Miley, on her life philosophy, interview with Hattie Collins, *Vogue*, June 4, 2021.